The Delphi Series
Volume VI

featuring

Allison Blevins
Saul Hillel Benjamin
Cameron Morse

Published by Blue Lyra Press

Copyright © 2019 BLUE LYRA PRESS
All rights reserved.

ISBN-13: 978-1-7338909-9-1
ISBN-10: 1-7338909-9-8
Blue Lyra Review, a journal of diverse voices, is a division of
Blue Lyra Press, and it is currently closed to new submissions.

Blue Lyra Press publishes several times a year and accepts poetry and flash fiction chapbook submissions under 25 pages during two months throughout each year: January and July only. Send directly to the email below.

Blue Lyra Review & *Blue Lyra Press* are independent and rely solely on the generosity of donations so **please** support the arts: (**www.bluelyrareview.com/donations/**).

SUBMISSIONS: direct to email with bio, acknowledgments, and table of contents

FACEBOOK: www.facebook.com/BlueLyraPress

TWITTER: twitter.com/MESilverman_BLP

PURCHASE: bluelyrapress.com/

CORRESPONDENCE: **bluelyrareview@gmail.com**

Front Cover: Robin Grotke's *Observing One Another*

Front Cover Design: Claire Zoghb

NOTE TO READERS

It is my delight to introduce you to the first book in the Delphi Series in a long time. After a long absence and the closing of our sister journal, *Blue Lyra Review,* we are proud to introduce three wonderful and deeply moving chapbooks. I hope you enjoy it as much as I do! This single bound book consists of three separate chapbooks by three separate poets bound in one single volume. Why would anyone do this? Good question! I think you, the reader, picked this book up because you are interested in one of the poets within these bound pages. In doing so, you are now exposed to two other poets. Maybe you heard of them before you picked this book up; maybe you didn't. It's like getting 3 books for the price of 1!

Allison Blevins begins the three chapbooks with a view into the innermost corners of love. The opening poem delves into love with beautiful lines like: "Inside her mouth, / we forget every ending." Blevins explores other subjects from feminism to laments, from abandonment to motherhood, as the reader truly revels in these soft murmurings that grip the reader and never let go. This chapbook is filled with little moments that explore these subjects, such as in "Birds": "The children and I celebrate the birds, / we spin our bodies through the air, our regrets / spin to shining, our arms cut circles in the air." In my favorite poem, "Everyone Waits at the DMV," Blevins writes: "Loving—the good bits— / is frantic scrambling for something you've misplaced." The poet captures an understanding of our inner most nature.

Saul Hillel Benjamin continues the theme of family and love in *Laud.* The opening poem, "At Summer's End," eloquently captures a common moment of apple picking into something larger and more universal. Benjamin writes: "In search of what we might become / we strip the summer down to seed.../ We steal what we already own." These poems celebrate fatherhood and love, weaving a sense of moving music in every poem. This can be seen in the sonnet which the chapbook is named after and concludes the book as well: "Love can be still, and be love, still." Benjamin knows how to turn a phrase, to create poems that are ultimately not just about love but about oneself. "You have / To go out into the world to find the world / Waiting inside yourself."

Cameron Morse bookends the series with lovely, sorrowful poems about his family and his personal fight with cancer. Morse writes: I "feared I wasn't really living." These are brave poems that force the reader to face hard truths. But ultimately, each poem is about family and both the beauty and comfort found within our loved ones. Morse stuns the reader with simplicity, with a matter-of-factness, such as in poems like "The Fitting" or "Shaving my Head". The mundane blossoms into so much more: "its dishes hot out of the washing machine, / the smell of laundry in the nostril / of the exhaust fan, a rusty spade left out in the rain." By the time the reader approaches the last poem, how can one not be moved to tears? "Nightfall came early for me, / too. I knew it was night when my shadow crawled / back into my body and a chill slipped / like black lace into the wind."

So, sit down with these three poets on a rocking porch chair. Or in a garden filled with birds.

Table of Contents

Susurration

by

Allison Blevins

For Mac and Lainey

Disclaimer

Table of Contents

Acknowledgments

Many thanks to the editors of the following magazines:

Eunoia: "Hedge Apples," "I Walk Down A Hall Toward the Building Elevator, The Sound of My Wife And Children Behind A Door At My Back," "If This Is Not A Memoir," and "Damned Women"
Green Hills Literary Lantern: "Baby Aubade"
Hastag Queer: LGBTQ+ Creative Anthology, Volume 2: "Daughter, What I've Learned," "My Daughter Returns from Her Other Mother's House with Braids in Her Hair," and "Femme Poem #1"
I-70 Review: "When Glass Breaks, The Cracks Move Faster Than 3,000 Miles Per Hour"
Josephine Quarterly: "Jar as Self Portrait"
Literary Mama: "Doorway of the Mother"
Mayday Magazine: "How to Be Gay In Missouri"
Pilgrimage: "Before the Storm, My Son Covers"
Sinister Wisdom: "How to Be Gay in Missouri"
Solidago Literary Journal: "Birds"
The Human: "Femme Poem #2"
the minnesota review: "The Body Is Not Ekphrastic"
the museum of americana: "Everyone Waits at the DMV"
The New Verse News: "After the Inauguration, Everything is Portentous"
Toad The Journal: "The Supreme Court Hears Oral Arguments Against Gay Marriage"

I am sincerely grateful for the help and encouragement of many writers and editors, especially Sally Keith, Claudia Rankine, Morri Creech, Alan Micheal Parker, Jon Pineda, Michelle Hendrixson Miller, Richard Allen Taylor, Greg Stapp, Julie Ramon, and everyone in the Publication Blitz.

Laura Lee Washburn, Roland Sodowsky, Chris Anderson, and Melissa Fite Johnson, thank you for all your Sunday afternoons and close reads.

Finally, thank you to Hannah.

"I thought we'd avoid the usual pitfalls because a man wasn't involved."
—Myla Goldberg

"And I say this: their beauty has more meaning / Than the whole human race and the race of birds."   —Robinson Jeffers

Susurration

i.
Woman full with a child is rocking all that she's grown
and done, all carried, like rocks,
soft moon shaped burdens. Like the flowing
and drowning river: woman and child.

ii.
The danger of overthinking is that
even on our bed I get lost between
the sheets and embroiled pillows. You on top
of me, the muscles in your arms stroke my ears.

iii.
A cello interrupts some days—no, not a cello—
the strings, lowing and drifting.
Only the strings, never the wood, never
fingers or a woman. Accept this.

iv.
You'll need this tune, the mother says. *You'll need
it for what comes next. Today is not
just any old . . . once you let go . . . child,
let go and tumbling follows.*

v.
I'm dying? My son asks. *You're dying.*
Obsessed. Every sneeze is dying.
The vitamin is dying. The cat is dying.
Broccoli too. *What will become of us?*

vi.
Memorize the sound of laughter
exploding from the mouth
of a lover at great distance: a clasp's
hook letting go of its eye.

vii.
My body was built for this. Inside her mouth,
we forget every ending. Fools.
Shut behind our bedroom door, we pretend
pain has never clawed our skin.

viii.
We Google the population of every town
we drive through. Significant somehow.
Relevant. At some point, you'll look for narrative.
You'll want to know who is *you.*

ix.
Crows lift off my back. A small silver bell
clears its throat, peals through the night.
A truck washes its feet. Accept the crows.
Accept the bell and mud.
                              Accept the pines
flinging off their needles, a carpet of brown shifting
in the breeze like strangers waiting.
Put all impermanence in your pocket.

x.
I found all of this in a crowded room,
bodies pressed in neat rows, the friction
of standing too close but not touching creates rhythm,
music, the ecstasy of raised hands clapping.

Louder than the bass or drums, the tune
of one voice, strangers connected as if
in prayer. Look at their faces turned towards light.
They sit and stand and sit. They bare their teeth.

How to Be Gay in Missouri

Keep watch over your children. Forget about linger and loaf. Think of all the yeses you've spoken. Aim to be small. Remember loving the sound of some place: a hum or a whoosh. When the men come, when they swell, chests puffed full of gospeled breath, let them come. Be broken like kindling. Remember your mother's perfume. Think of the hills, deep and lasting. Keep watch over your feet. Slink into the cracks in the sidewalk. Be mud.

Birds

Blackbirds flock the milo, a heart shaped fog.
The children and I chase. The birds leave.
Return. Their wings cut strokes through the sky
between the pear and our volunteer milo.
The children and I feel the chill of their wings
as a hunger. We know secrets wait for us inside.
My wife's threats still dust the kitchen floor. We stay outside.
We press our faces against the glass panes
in the front door, trace stars in the fog from our breath.
The children and I flap our arms. We swim
along the grass. Hardening and browning,
the grass forgets our flaws. The grass is a kindness,
incapable of blame. The children and I celebrate the birds,
we spin our bodies through the air, our regrets
spin to shining, our arms cut circles in the air.

The Body Is Not Ekphrastic

One in four Americans lives within three miles
of a toxic waste dump. The body asks how far is far enough.
Self-immolation seems the only sane choice, the body
transubstantiated to liquid fat, flame
the message and the messenger. Close your eyes.

What makes you angry? A person you've never met
loading a gun, deliberately not thinking of you?
Children remembering their unblemished bodies,
their bodies unzipped? Close your eyes.
Smell the sulfur on the water. All women
are a one in eight chance of breast cancer,
the body a representation of risk,
disease the message and the messenger.

The body loves anger more than living.
You wouldn't ask birds to stop flocking like fish,
like choreographed machinery.
Listen to the body. Violence is justified.
The body wants to refuse breath
and drink, think of ways to become a bomb.

Close your eyes: the body as ultrasonic image,
fingerlike projections reach out to cup ducts,
love as parasite, love as leaching.
If bodies have souls, we know
what cancer is eating. The body
finds voice remembering the doctor
calling just to say: *Your cells have breached the margins.*

Baby Aubade

Evening was less simple before our son
was between us, mouth on my breast
suckling in a dream. I wish I could stop
sleep, watch the stars again
through cigarette smoke. I miss that
dusky black, the before, before our breath
swirled air ripe with sour milk and urine.
We watched the sun rise over chain links
perspiring day, the sun interrupted
groping, tongues whipping mouths,
and smoke dragged the light over our thighs
and hands tangled like webs. We don't wait now,
for the rise, the good orange morning.
We know only sleep and the soft
exhalation hanging between us.

Separation

Here, our faces pressed against the glass. Here,
my flaws on your lips. *I'm fond of my flaws*

on your lips. Here a short drum beat, a yellow
traffic sign: slow. Here we wrapped our smiling arms

around every tree. Here the days burned
regret into our bodies, our bodies like dust.

Here I open my unspeakable body to check the organs
slowly shaping into stone. Here is the red dress

stained with *I love you.* Here is my waiting and every night
you never return. Here are airport lights.

I want to reach. *I do.* Here another woman
behind another door. Our children sleep.

I know just how life would have felt,
growing old with you still loving me.

If This is Not a Memoir

Consider. A leaf falls from a tree. Does this mark the beginning of descent? I'd prefer to tell this story as fiction: A girl erases her own name from a blackboard, writes her name again. Her room is not windy, no chalky billows, no dust stuck like burrs to the backs of chairs. All year the oaks sing, give voice to the body's suffering. What part of my body is important to any of you? Everyone is worried about themselves: we don't shake hands, you don't put two fingers inside me, you don't inhale the narrative from my mouth, you don't feel how every exhalation becomes a metaphor. This is not a metaphor. It is not my voice that sings. Call the words fiction. Call me an oak.

Damned Women

Each morning my friend calls to check
on me. I tell this dying woman I want to die.
My hair trembles. I tell this dying woman
that my children can no longer see my face,
that love looks like an egg cracking.

       My son's breath blows into my mouth
       each night. My daughter still wakes
       screaming for her mother who abandoned us.

Do you think each body's death
was inscribed in the lining of our marrow?
Cancer, my friend's inscription reads.
She is alone. This is the middle.
The beginning was a lump in her breast.

       Months after we decide to divorce,
       the children and I still run solitary circles
       in the browning grass. Chiggers ride the motion
       of our steps waving the blades. The children
       are breaking me with their beauty.

Together our mouths shape loss,
and it sounds like *ohs* stamped out
behind solid oak doors. Loss is shut out of sight,
like women and starving and bleeding
and the shimmer of water draining.

My Daughter Returns from Her Other Mother's House with Braids in Her Hair

Another woman's twists undo themselves
between my fingers. I become like silence,
caught in the gaps. In the slow shadow of evening,
the children and I relearn each other
after our night as separate bodies. Their breath and fingers
sneak into my clothes. I mouth into their fleshy crooks.
My daughter's hair, kinked
by some other woman, slips wild down her back,
gallops after her down the hall. We laugh like insomniacs.

The Supreme Court Hears Oral Arguments Against Gay Marriage

When my wife abandoned our children,
their chests fluttered each night in my bed
like new leaves peeking from still forming branches.

If I stand in our yard and tilt my head back,
I can smell the honeysuckle just beginning.
All of this is tender.
                        Think of how a petal oozes
after it is crushed. Think of the liquid,
gluey and coating the spirals. Then you are with me
in this moment. My life flashes like a child's plastic stereoscope.

My pumping heart defines the moment as human,
not like a metronome but a screen, maybe circular
and revolving. And yes. This is disorienting,

this ever-spinning stage, all true as the tearing of birth,
as the fresh green blood of something raw
coming into a room for the first time.

Femme Poem #1

Greened and kernelled and rowed, the prairies suffer
the artifice of summer: the pruning and plucking, the machinery, the
finery.

> Everything you see is a lie: curls and brows, powders and potions,
> the work of woman. If I took off my skin, rolled the flesh down
> mandible and ulna, you would see truth in my exposed gristle.

Wild with weeds, unrowed for a few cold months,
field becomes prairie again and breathes.

> Hiding inside me is a mohawk, a buzz, a low pony:
> Tumble out baseball glove, knees apart, flannel, leather boots,
> workman's pants, white tank, solid stride, wallet on a chain.

The farmer's children trace shapes in the stars, warm backs pressed
into sharp winter grass, love uncovered.

> Many days, I want to trade my safety, my mascara and heels,
> for all the world's glorious *sirs* and all its disapproving glances.

Daughter, What I've Learned

To answer your question, I'd have to point
to Kansas on a map: Here's where we began.
The house and doors and walls are so much bigger
when you force your cheek against the carpet.
Here's where a body must know when to go limp.

We were just people you'll never know.
Restless girls, we spread our legs,
knees crooked like arms akimbo.
Our bodies pleased with being flung.

We were young before the graceless years,
before the counting stones filled jar after jar,
before the filled stone jars stacked in every corner.

When Glass Breaks, the Cracks Move Faster than 3,000 Miles Per Hour

Once, her son stopped breathing. She saw her arms,
sedate and thick, around his shoulders, felt her own breath
as a burden forcing her into a chair. As a girl,

she knew love was like 10,000 small and desperate boxes,
knew her body, now marble and smooth, would one day
turn jagged and home would feel like stone pressed

too long into the shoulder of a rocky shore. She doesn't know
anything about the human heart but that a lover's smell lingers
in her shirt long after they've left her bed. She watched

a man die once. He reached out his arms as if begging
the room to shrink, as if he wanted her to touch her fingers
to the small hollows of his feet, as if he knew

he had smelled the scent of another person for this one last time.

Jar as Self-Portrait

A jar filled with reddening leaves sits
outside a door. An empty jar warbles
in a low wind as if its base were an ellipse
tuned to spin.
                  Peel the label from a jelly jar.
Soak in vinegar. Scrub glue residue.
Store in the cabinet until there's need
of juice or water.
                  A jar tips, spills its insides.
A jar shatters from liquid bubbling
in the center. A jar glides along water run down
its side, glides like an invisible hand desires
the jar moves slightly to the right.
                              A jar fills
and empties. Think of church on Sunday,
a parking lot, think of a breast, a bladder,
a woman, a mouth, a tank, a bowl,
your thrumming, thrumming heart.

Femme Poem #2

Every woman I've loved is a man.
Women who shake their hair like men,
palm my lower back, wear their jeans low.

All that I love is delicate, petals on a bough:
a strong tongue in a female mouth,
men's trousers on curved hips in a men's bathroom stall.

I want to say this is masculinity
done right. This is a hand on my throat
without the anticipation of being crushed

beneath the buckle of a belt . . . my father's belts.
Neat. Belts in black and brown rows.
I want to say I love a woman

as a man in a woman's body,
a woman in a body made hard and lean,
a body made to glow in the reflection

of all the lamplight eyes glaring
as she walks down the street.
I fear you will hear:

I want a man. I just know what I want—
boxer briefs hugging a woman's legs, musk,
and the stink of armpits I'd want to lose myself in.

Before the Storm, My Son Covers

his ears against the wind, our walk
interrupted by the clapping hysteria of ash,
the cackling of oaks. My son refuses
the trail, his feet and the dirt, acorn and crunch,
for my arms. I want to explain the lesson here:
how trunks groan and limbs speak, the purpose
of decay, how we crush beauty
beneath our boots, how he should give
his heart to the birds. But we turn
together toward the car. I run
as rains beat down on our heads
pressed cheek to cheek. He sees dirt
become mud. He sees the pattern
of my steps stamped out in retreat.

After the Inauguration, Everything is Portentous

I think about absolutes of motion when I'm naked,
how a pendulum swings, how a scale unbalanced
must wobble, how my skin ripples, weight unsteadies.

Something alive is buzzing in the kitchen, leg
against leg, string against bow, like the sound
of nothing, boxed and electrified. Blackness

circles the sky above my son's school most afternoons.
I want to say *blackness* as if dawn or waking from sleep
or blood rising to air were sinister, but the feeling

on my skin is more like dust, fine and granular, settling
even in my throat. I could say the circling and flapping
and cawing will alight as sediment, in the corners,

in the morning, after God has closed his eyes,
after God has opened them again. Because my children
don't notice my body unclothed, when I walk naked,

I am emperor. I parade the living room, parade
this boulevard of blind children. The images we steep in
are invisible. On the playground at my son's school

children in puffed and quilted jackets gather and ring
around a solitary boy. The children silent, the boy's mouth
buzzes. All the feathers, dark and rustling, fall from above.

I Walk Down a Hall Toward the Building Elevator, the Sound of My Wife and Children Behind a Door at My Back

If I say my wife leaving was a fall from a height
of little consequence to the body, except my lungs
compressed and faltering in the invisible science
of ending, this would be true. Also,
this would be a lie. My poems leave nothing
to unravel: We are lovers out of love.
No secrets wait in the darkened hallway
of my hardening veins. These bodies have nothing
to spill for you. My wife leaving means each step
becomes simply walking. Every glance
at her face means I'm intruding
on my life, yet she still drags me behind her
coupled train cars rattling in the cold.

Everyone Waits at the DMV

Breath, cottony and damp, poured into your mouth
from another mouth. Lowing strings fill silences.
This sound must be a cello. On a road not empty,
not dark or untread, every passerby is a stranger,
all the lights red and blinking. A floor so glossy

it doesn't seem to touch any feet but reflects:
a poster, a clock. Some may feel their bodies reverse.
So we are. A white-haired caterpillar on the back
of a hand wades the hairs like flood water.
Leaves turn orange and burn too early or too late

and our memory of exactly when somehow always lost.
A child dies. So we are. Unvoiced conversations
spoken through the widening and narrowing
whites of eyes across a room. Fly in the house.
Ants on the baseboard. Water, cold and weeping,

walked to the sofa by a lover or mother. Suspect
on the loose. Close the windows. A chill in our guts.
So we are. Endings are like lowering your own body
onto something wet and crumbling. Loving—the good bits—
is frantic scrambling for something you've misplaced.

Commuting

How much of this world has meaning simply as beauty:
a biplane flies low, ditch weeds overtake
a row of electrical poles, my own mascaraed eyes
look up at it all? My lashes are a facade,
woman as doe as portrait of woman looking up
as if innocent. I've been told I have that look in my eye.

Even the buildings, neon and plaster facade,
reach out to interrogate me. I'm not certain
any longer what is love or what is love
wholly absent from an embrace. The woman
across from me at dinner last night forgot
to eat, so lost in the delicious promise of me.

Rebellion is the anticipation of a woman
inside me. In that moment, I've no need
but my own gray ache, no pears to quarter,
no small hands tugging, no sleeves tacked
with snot and juice. My fingers embraced
by a woman's skin, I am more than just-a-mother.

Something to hold in my hand, my daughter cries now
each morning. This is how she fills herself: a small baby doll,
a plastic kitty she calls baby. Her hands clutch
two small toys, she stumbles and forgets to catch herself
on the stairs. I think of those Wisconsin winters
the electrical poles caught fire, something to do with earth and salt.

She never cried, my wife. So easy to forget how
we watched the children trample leaves every fall,
not yet knowing the weight of broken bodies.
I've been told to stop writing my regrets.
I promise, but each night the pen writes
grief as if *grief* was the only word left.

When I'm finally gone, I'll no longer carry
the weight of every touch I thought worth living for
as a stone. Some people you carry forever, a burden
of feathers brined to your cheeks. My date slipped silent
from my bed this morning, leaving only the certainty
that no grown hands will touch any part of me for days.

Hedge Apples

Mothers once placed Osage Oranges under their babies' beds to repel spiders.
Martha Stewart recommends quartering, drying, displaying at Christmas.

The old woman tells me: Keep what you love.
Place the fruit in every corner of every room.
Quarter the fruit. Relish the milky burst.
Don't quarter the fruit.
                      Let your impossible burdens
brown in every closet. Let the boughs splinter
and drop. Keep the fruit whole.
Make a barrier of green before every door.
Keep the skin dusty.
                    Press the ridges to your tongue.
Savor the weight of every choice
in your hand like motherhood swelling your belly.
She tells me to search the eastern tree line.
I crawl the length of barbed wire—bramble, ivy
and fear—to hold my impossible love near.

Doorway of the Mother

A mother on fire sits up and smiles through the flames.
I will be with you wherever I go.

A mother under the knife cups nothing in her hands.
You are made of me. You are dawn
and wind and dirt climbing free
from the earth. You are made of me.

A mother squeezes the arms tight, too tight.
I need a minute. Please. Just.
Be quiet. For a minute.

A mother unfolding her hands clenches her teeth.
Some muscle in her body must be tight as horses running.
This is my mouth. This is my brow.
These are my fingers crooked
and ugly at the first knuckles.

A mother tells a stranger that this is not her child—
some are bound to never know where they are going.
You are bluer than the moon.
You are bluer than the river.
You are the best I have ever done.

A mother dances, stomps. A mother
dances like a saxophone taps.
I carry your heart. I've eaten your heart.
I've eaten myself eating your heart. Don't worry.
I gather your tears and eat those too.

A mother was a child once without love. She calls the earth a person.
In the beginning, no one needed to be told how to become a person.
I cannot undress our ending, soften
the panic of loss. If you stand
as evening in forgiveness of the day—
it's like that. It's like that, child.

Author's Bio

Allison Blevins received her MFA at Queens University of Charlotte and is a Lecturer for the Women's Studies Program at Pittsburg State University and the Department of English and Philosophy at Missouri Southern State University. Her work has appeared in such journals as *Mid-American Review, the minnesota review, Nimrod International Journal, Sinister Wisdom,* and *Josephine Quarterly.* She is the author of the chapbooks *Letters to Joan* (Lithic Press, 2019) and *A Season for Speaking* (Seven Kitchens Press, 2019), part of the Robin Becker Series. She lives in Missouri with her wife and three children where she co-organizes the Downtown Poetry reading series and is Editor-in-Chief of *Harbor Review.* http://www.allisonblevins.com.

Laud

by

Saul Hillel Benjamin

For Noah, who taught me how to sing

Table of Contents

Acknowledgments

The following poems have been previously published or presented, and the author is grateful to the magazines and venues which first welcomed them:

The American Oxonian: "When Autumn Comes to Broadway & Maiden Lane"
The American Scholar: "At Summer's End"
FM 107.1 Winnipeg: "Laud", "Quill", "Stradivarius, Singing"
The Poetry Society of Great Britain: "Stradivarius at Ninety-Three",
    "Stradivarius Prepares for the Feast"
The San Diego Poetry Anthology 2019: "Tracks, Everywhere"
Sewanee Writers Conference: "The Marriage Stanzas", "The Anniversary of
    Everyday",
The Vice Chancellor's 2016 International Poetry Prize Anthology: "December
    Weather"
The Vice Chancellor's 2017 International Poetry Prize Anthology: "Almost
    Equinox"

For the tenacity and guidance (too often disregarded by its recipient) of their friendship, I voice particular thanks: Nan Coiner, David Quammen, Barry and Erica Goode, HT, Doc Wally, Sollace Mitchell, Marvin Krislov, Carter and Katrina Brandon, David Hicks, Daniel Mark Epstein, Doug Eakeley, Sir Rick and Lady Marguerite, Jon Friesen, Jill Kearney, and Ilka Threimer. And with vivid memory of Donald Pogue, Darryl Gless, Tom O'Brien, Frank Allen, Delayne Barber, Jean Floud, Tom Mikula, Laura Knudsen, Christoffel Coetzee, Louie the Pencil, Don and Beth Straus, and Robert Penn Warren.

At Summer's End

Months of waiting: then everyone
clamoring down the hill
       to the orchards for its meats.
   Winter long, rooted
snug in bed with books

up to our armpits, we plotted
summer's populations:
       the musty peach, the sex
  of pears; the sorbs and apples.
Amulets for our mouths to dream.

Differences are what count.
I can tell by the actual thump
       whether it's an apple
  or a sorb that's hit the path
or the soft or hard ground.

Apples recite: delicious, sweet.
Sorbs are blunt.
       Some of us need ladders,
  but others have only
to reach for what they need.

Lowest branches deliver up
their goods with least objection.
       But even topmost fruits fall down
  to mumble from our wooden crates.
Delicious bitter, delicious red.

Then falling light: the mind at war.
In search of what we might become
       we strip the summer down to seed,
  and lug our thieving up the hill.
We steal what we already own.

The Falls at Otter Creek

If we think of how
things might have gone
we've already missed the point.
Here, nothing is over
even if the differences
continually tempt

more satisfying
explanations. After all,
that's the reason

we've come here again
and again: expecting
the perennial display

might demonstrate
our capacity to overcome
the permanence of change.

Instead, we're left
to marvel at
the troubling symmetry:

shadows migrating
with startled sunfall,
declaring the arc

that measures the shape
of rock that crafts
the cataract: like words

adrift headlong
down the looming
chute of vapors

rising only to see
our trophies scorned
by gravity

and then lift straight
up, incited past
our jealous fingertips

to argue memory's
hold we cannot keep:
weighty things

like friendship or marriage
those fragile architects
of circumstance and hope

whose every claim
we both doubt and desire
taken so easily

too lightly, we always
risk assumptions:
this is how things are

or *this* is how they'll remain.
But here at Otter Creek
in the first approaches

to springtime we invent
our own necessities.
Where we stand

an uncertain ledge
disputes last year's
certainties: shale

giving way to quartz
or metamorphic;
persistence nudged

now here, now there.
We dare to keep
what we doubt to trust.

Our footing fails:
we shift costly weight
and stumble past

our broken faith.
Sunlight sings and breaks
the freighted edge

of guarded truths
that hold us back.
Nothing is ever over:

patterns of damage
and acceptance
tell us who we are.

We fall and rise
into unexpected lives.
And falling, reach.

Rising, Too Early, Monday Morning

When it's late at night and branches
are banging against the window
in the perch of our nesting room

I find myself thinking (or is it only
plotting) that love is like leaping
out of the frying pan of oneself

into the fire of someone else.
But it's of course more complicated
than that, or not complicated at all.

It's more like trading two scarlet birds
arguing in the prickled bush outside
for the one, refusing, in your hand.

It's certainly not as simple as just
getting up on the wrong side of the bed
boasting blue shorts with yellow starfish

for the reason that a little boy delights
to imagine how the ocean could be
sailing across his Papa's underwear.

It's more like the way a postponed pen
parries then defeats the sword
of self-snaring brittleness. Or

the way that a penny found or the ninth
dropped stitch, somehow, gets reinvested.
Through the halo of the rising day

there's everything and little else to say.
Except that the road, turning ahead,
is what the early bird, rising, begs

to remind: that even when shadows
tremble on the walls or darken corners,
love is, ever, better late than never.

Lines While Cleaning Dishes

If in my mind I marry you daily
It's to calm an extravagance of love
with sobering custom, for it flames
each day's chores that only you and I
would bother to count or record.

After all, what does it matter if dishes
pile up and require rearrangement;
or books, mis-stacked here and there, call out
for order's re-shelving; or socks, divorced
from pairs, stranded wait for reunion?

If in my heart I marry you each day
it's not anniversary's reckoning sight.

But simplicity's extravagance: each day's
common rising: daily life, daily life.

The Anniversary of Everyday

To keep loving where wonderfully
We once ached in love is not easy.
Evidence of promises turned unkindly
Or thwarted; or worse, emptied
By overuse, getting put aside
In the tedious swale of laundry
Or anger, lost bus tickets and diapers.

There really ought to be rules:
The way we have rules for putting the knife
To the left (or is it the right?) of the plate
On which we carry burdens of recipes
Savored but never adequately praised,
Or concoctions better left in the sink.

Goodness knows, there are years like days
When all it's possible to do is simply
To keep loving, letting anger teach.
To hope in silence, cleaning the sink.
But mostly, just mostly, to praise.

Outside, a child cheers and plots
immortality, while cicadas,
heedless, whirr and strum
Worlds we dream, worlds we lose.

No foreknowledge of autumn
Keeps from steadfast enterprise.
What's found is lost, troubled

Like everything too
Carefully put away

For safe-keeping.

December Weather

I thought today I should write the truth
about love, especially since so many
others have had their say but left me
unsatisfied, still figuring it out.

      So I went into the woods, winter's
      chill everywhere hanging from tangled
      limbs, and hoped to feel, well you know,
      inspired or maybe sort of religious.

 stood about for a while, kicking
a stone lodged between a rock and another
hard place, but I slipped on ice, the way
we often lose our way in memory.

      My feet stiffened. I began to worry
      that I'd left my best socks on the bedroom
      floor, and in the rush to tell the truth
      Had put on wrong ones for serious work.

That's when I realized that we're not,
you know, getting any younger. Hardly
the kind of uplift that the truth about
anything is really after, after all.

      But that's also when it came to me
      that we're not getting older either.
      And just about that time, I heard
      a scattered crew of geese overhead.

Maybe they were Canadian, but wintry
glare makes it hard to tell. Maybe they were
elsewhere from or bound, flocking loyally,
steadfast through ice and rain, homeward.

       I would almost swear (which is a kind
       of vow, after all) that two of them
       were trailing raucous colored scarves;
       one of them, quite stylishly.

It made me remember that it's cold
today and lonely without you, always.
Though, sometimes, it's lonely with you.
That's also part of lovestruck's truth:

       Needing to get away into the woods;
       just so that, coming back, I'll bring homeward
       a broken limb or branch, weighted down
       with the loyalty of our including hearts.

The Marriage Stanzas

Nothing not dared, everything tempted.
Wearing pomegranate and crimson,
Romping in hues of teasing vermillion:
One night we parried tongues, hands, teeth…
But you only get so much time, and clocks
Are not built for perpetual rewinding.
Those days language itself was the dance.
We quoted, exhausted, the three famous words:
As if telling somebody they're loved
Was defense against currency's chance.

I knew a voluptuous-mouth poet
Whose haberdashery of sunflower blue
And yellow cravats issued lengthy laments:
Last night's certainties, morning's retake.
Dizzied verse stranding its aphrodisiac,
Ambitious to figure everything out.

Once, I toddled up a hill and came down,
With the threat of a thousand-page manuscript.
Each syllable savvy, each couplet well-hung.
Art, everybody knows, is tough work.
But I'm tired of dancing, I really am.
Would anybody mind if I just sat still
And pictured the sweet industry of bees,
Plotting from root to stamen to flower?
My trousers are not rolled. I'm not old:
I just like trousers pleated quadruple.

Take from settled history quarrels we must.
We need not be pawns in some ancient tryst:
Let's make the bed and sit in a garden,
Ours or borrowed, surrounded by the dull
Hum of bees. What *was* that dance we enjoyed
Between perfection and its fierce verdict?

I think it was the rhythm of a question:
Asked not answered, a turn of willing ear
Towards the prospect of insight shared.
It's hard not fleeing tomorrow's comfort
When you're stricken by yesterday's loss.
Knowing remembers before memory believes.
But nothing remembered is ever over.
To music we've never heard, let's dance
Yet-found names we can only guess.
Desiring everything, lucky with less.

Stradivarius, Singing

With gifts of muslin
      and pebbled onyx,

the stone that steals
      the light it makes,

I wake to find you
      pitched above me:

out of instinct,
      out of practice,

the taste of resin
      swimming in your throat.

Summer to frost, then to ice:
      January clangs its iron door.

O, Love, take heart
      when chill offends

or harsh winds drum
      resistance from

our challenged trust:
      remember how

this night we've sung
      in myriad tongues.

Stradivari Prepares for the Feast of the Virgin

Dear Lady, you know that I have lately
Purchased an estate in fee simple
      In Ostia. I beg you to preserve
           The two provinces of Lombardy
    And Ostia from earthquake and fire.

As I have also a mortgage
At Tuscany, I petition further
      An eye of compassion
           On that province. As for the rest:
    You may deal with them as you please.

Times are hard; even so, I have set,
In my own namesake, a fund for orphans.
      Sweet Lady, enable the banks
           To answer all their bills, and make
    My debtors good and honest men.

And assure a prosperous voyage
And return to the sloop *Caritas*
      Whose transit I have not insured.
           Finally, since it is written "the days
    Of the wicked are short", I trust

You will honor that hopeful teaching.
I have an estate in reversion
      To settle upon me with the censure
           Of that profligate, Guarneri,
    Who fiddles no honest trade.

Stradivarius Dines Alone

Is it the double-stopped chord
That beckons, or the fortress-mount
Of her sumptuous offering: lying
                    Resigned before me,
An *arpeggio* of risotto peas?

Or the choice meat itself: soft
As an angel's thigh beckoning
A menu I'll never digest, but
                    Only parse, like Heaven's
Clarion *trattoria*'s craft?

Or questing a darkened corner:
Will she step, brazen, and take a seat
Aching just inches from desire
                    And issue thwarted words
I crave: *Piacere*, your wish?

But instead of her, sated, I enter
The marrow that is the secret
No truffled menu sequestered
                    Reveals: *You may savor*
And tip. You may taste, but never keep.

In any case, it's just the night shift.
She's gone to another: *Piacere?*
After the first course, what do you wish?
                    Or do you prefer
We go direct to summoning sweets?

Stradivarius, Remembering Kudzu

Your life thieves mine.
Why conspire ungenerous
Dancing so wanton,
Ensnared by fierce truths
Smarter angels refuse?
I'm asking, just asking.
I don't know what you'll plot
Or self-preserving extract
From snares we've invented.
The timepiece at your throat
Was a Michaelmas gift.
We were immortal: like
Everyone raptured
Beyond doubt's calendar.

I strap my Father's wrist-watch

On my wedding's shred hand:
The kind that requires, turn
By turn, hard rewinding.
Ironic, given staggering
Debts of pocket and oaths.
Even so, *his* vows had
Longer shelf-life. How
Have we've come to this?
Trapped in kudzu's
Strangle: one hungering
Safety, the other striving.
Shouldn't this be easier?
Shouldn't release sing
Something, finally, like joy?

Almost Equinox

The year not quite on its hinge, I want
To speak about the happiness of my body
And the delight its joints exert when climbing
Three-hundred-and-forty-two stairs to reach
The pedestrian boardwalk on the eastward side
Of the Arno's cobbled rise where sunshine
Exuberant pours from azure seamless skies.

The sun rides in sweeps of scarlet finery,
Indifferent to my swift joy as rightly
That's how it works. So, step by stride I follow
A queue of mothers pushing signature
Prams carting future fiddlers bleating squeals
Of laughter from eastward westward until
Even my sorrow tires hearing itself.

Though I've been scorned for it, let me never
Be afraid to use the word *beautiful* or *hope*
Or any other flowers in the garden of voice.
Just now a hummingbird --- I swear it's true ---
Has drummed its trumpet's brilliant engine
Literally across my path and swerved
Back again as if to show the way home.

How many days did the boy I was never
Speak the holy words of gratitude or grace
Yet all the while believed I surely had?
Shame upon that captive boy's successor
For thwarted years that might have flourished.
But that, too, is how it works. You have
To go out into the world to find the world

Waiting inside yourself: to rescue (from false
Because empty certainties) the bravery
Waiting to speak, waiting to be heard.
Not *too* many words, mind you, just enough
To honor the sun rising or later the frogs
Incanting bodily happiness from mud
Naming resolute waters, ever flowing below.

The Creation of the World

Whatever else, there must be music.
Searing, brilliant; intent, intentional.
Like mathematics and its implacable
Declarations: everything is perfect.
No work to be done, no vows, no Sabbath
To celebrate beyond the intrinsic
Joy that is every day's anniversary.
The geometer cannot demonstrate
The beauty of lines; they are not his concern.
Nor the luthier the consequence of craft.
Enough, simply, to witness and enact.
  Risk all, risk all.

So, take this lute to hold and put pears
Whose flesh is scarred by the knife's hard edge
On a welcoming table, the plate and knife
In their proper places, an ordinary glass,
Not full but not empty, ready at hand.
Dress auburn ribbons in your thick curls
And tell me what you've always, reluctant
But steadfast, hungered to declare: that here
In the summer of our uncreated world
There is everything holy without cause.
Profusion, grateful, from astonished hands.
  Play on, play on.

Stradivarius at Ninety-Three

I knew each line, each curve: the flamed scroll
      and intricate head that issued key and pitch
  of all our efforts, the slightly arched neck

I spent hours climbing. I knew the breast
      of maple, the rib of spruce: the signature
  of sound that shaped our voice, incited breath.

And I knew the hidden wounds (my fingers
      traced each patch of surgery, each scar) and yet,
  for that, we hardly know each other now.

Our practice rattles a wooden death.
      A summer's desertion works its damage:
  tension is loosed, split strings cannot sing.

You fail the touch to which you leapt.
      A stupid warmth is all my hands now lend:
  I take your light body, noteless, to mine.

The Red Bandana

for Jacob Samuel Benjamin

The name of the ship your mother sailed
to Ellis Island ninety four years ago
was already long forgotten when you asked

what it had been like to travel eight
days in the dark and imagine a life
without fear because your name itself

gave strangers a reason for hatred,
and wonder if ever there'd be the comfort
of leavened bread or salt or safety.

That's the same story remembered
by your children who know even less
about how their father understood the days

of his life with a father who worked
with his hands and a mother who died
too young from malice or carelessness

leaving only the fragrance of her name.
What you remembered and told
was the story you said your mother told

about a young boy on a Hamburg steamer
who stopped a twelve year old from crying
and wiped her mouth with a red bandana,

pronouncing, slowly and often, the strange
word "mango", as its tart mercy ran
down the throat of a girl startled by hope.

She traveled, alone, with a single suitcase
and an address written in Yiddish
on a yellowed piece of packing paper

just the way that years later her son,
speaking aloud two syllables of a name
at her gravestone in Brooklyn, would find

that memory is something you eat, again
and again, while its verdict spills over
your chin, rooting in quarreled ground.

When Autumn Comes to Broadway and Maiden Lane

September 12ᵗʰ

Everywhere the signs are rising: chores
Of definition are what we are about.
Experts rush and counsel; relentless

About the obvious: and possibly, it helps.
But rainfall and star showers: these
Are what we seek, different braveries

To lift the brick and molten glass,
The burnt confetti of bone and steel
That stings the air our hearts inhale.

For us other autumns will rise: days
Of clarity, possibly graced. For now,
We must risk ourselves to find ourselves.

Standing, without you, at the barricade
Of Broadway and blooded Maiden Lane
I am lost: without a map.

Except that you are also stumbling
Or perhaps searching for a version
Of a compass to steer us by.

Is it apricot or bergamot whose taste
In my mouth lingers from yours
Or perhaps just memory's ache,

More fierce than facts, more tenacious
Than hope, that tests an uncertain
Season with foolish certainties?

What I know is little, but it is this:
Somewhere, west of urban shatter,
Cathedral rocks fill with flowering quince

And scarlet brush parades temptations
More brave than you or I would risk.
Near, though out of present reach,

A cardinal trills its tune: beckoned,
As if to claim what neither facts nor hope
Have rights upon, but yet might teach.

After Bregenz, Snowfall

My father vexed and chanted obituaries.
       Loss beyond metrics: maps, denoting.

As a child, I received monthly itineraries
       From *Esso Travel Service*. Tempting

Half-inch underlined blue markings: vintage
       Diners, signature landmarks, predicted

Redemptions beyond my *barrio* limits.
       But I'd never witness Lubbock

Or Gravel Switch or Medicine Hat
       Or endless other absurd-named delights.

Syllables, inscribed in blue, would suffice.
       But we finally wake, we always wake:

Rage beyond metrics, questions past voice.
       One day, for me, it was Bregenz.

Forty-eight years before, Europe's crossroad:
       Vile-drenched, boot-scarred, shirted-brown.

First, they come for your neighbor
       On the right and you calmly pull down

Your Venetian blinds. Next, it's the elder
       Couple on the left who left you *latkes*

With a dollop of nutmeg. They were
       Cattle-shipped to the unutterable.

What happens when they come for the rest:
       No neighbors left, witnesses bereft?

Late to Fatherhood, predictions quaver.
    Each morning, I steadfast climb down

Vexed stairs in breaking dark and return
    With heaping bowls of Irish cut oats.

We trust a haunted world cannot defeat.
    Will I do better for him than done to me?

What prowess of heart against tangled risk
    Will I summon to vouch his safety?

Noah, By Happenstance in Manitoba

I wake to winter's repetitions:
bankrupt horizon, cloudless; learning
how to count, without benefit.

But you'll sleep until nubs of growth
tenacious as first love, decide to push
an unfinished length upright,

expectant at the year's half-hinge,
roiling in the sweet counting tide.
East of the moon, north of the sun:

you'll have to begin in this least
of anywhere's desired setting,
by happenstance in Manitoba.

Years ago, on angered ground
called Holy by those who trespass
its praise, your mother learned to count.

Everything waits to be counted:
grizzled elders, wrapped or crowned
in *ghutras* or *yarmulkes* or competing

versions of *keffiyehs*. Children
equally Abraham's, hunkered down
now as then in stone alleyways, waiting

to avoid or answer a summons,
or brazenly dodge RPGs
or other cruel stupidities.

Numbers, everywhere: syllables
screaming at each other in separate
invested tongues, justification

for whatever is honored or scorned.
After all, it's what you'd expect:
everything counted doesn't always count.

Except love, too smart to argue
precinct equations. You could be born
anywhere, quarreled or beloved ground.

Stop counting: imagine instead
each day's summation. Springtime
beneath ice, waiting north of the sun.

Tracks, Everywhere

Everywhere any two lines run, no matter
      How improbably across a carpet's
   Inscribed triple-stitched *fleur-de-lis*

Or the seams in an orange or a crack
      In the sidewalk, my son harbors
   No doubts that trains are, somehow, singing.

Northbound or southbound or tugged
      By other compass scheduled bearings,
   All routes arm against instructed sleep.

The world invites interpretation;
      Demands it in fact: so why not accept
   That every line ahead leads backwards

To its tempted future? Darling, I once
      Walked with my Father at the scruff
   Edge of a railroad crossing in the midst

Of our *barrio* precinct, patient to chronicle
      As many prime numbers the *Frisco &*
   Santa Fe in its twilight calendar

Threw across our troubled partnership.
      Your Grandfather rails forever
   Without his wife, the Grandmother

You'll never meet, in a field crowded
      With fallen poppies and asphodel.
   Their lives bore numbers: an *abacus*

Of blooded thefts inscribed on forearms;
      Signatures that music dares not sing.
   Everywhere, everywhere: there are tracks.

My wounded Father never sang to me.
  Or at any rate his notes and clefs
 Are too long unheard to summon.

But I recall a star-empty night
  When drunk as usual with the anger
 Of a thwarted life, even so he coaxed

A battered harmonica from a drawer
  And whistled protecting tenderness
 To waltz his silent watchful boy.

Quill

for Noah

Hearing the wind striding towards us
From its tempting horizon, the great
Open spaces of Manitoba greet

Squadrons of geese navigating south.
I skirmish the kaleidoscope of years.
But you fasten on chores of dressing.

Overcoats stuffed against latitude
Only frenzied meteorologists delight.
Too varied our weather shoes to choose.

Darling boy, it's reckless as we lust
The vast mandala of our testing world
How we trafficked hope and loss and trust.

But late to fatherhood I exclaimed
At your first breath the syllable *Quill*.
It seemed right to plainly declare.

Each of us is stardust, so why not pluck
From ancient distances a single vow?
Look up that night ahead that I am gone:

That day you'll give it back, the weight
I wished I'd not carried so badly,
Leaving you instead to better portage.

Darling boy, darling boy: strive and feel
In recollected breath's sweet lightness
That even though by then I've vanished

I gave you worth each anchored day:
In your heart, in your heart, unaltered
Into the claiming dark, when I'm away.

Laud

Love, word-quiet: speak softly
and earn your place
    in heraldries of touch and taste.
        Love can be still, and still be love.

Love, word-eager: sing plainly
but without haste
    the best of measure's hopeful trait.
        Love can be still, and still be love.

Love, heart-ready: ask simply
of a world that's poised
    with simple proof if absent voice;
        pivots of breath, a pause, a will:

So near heart's hub they hardly stir.
        Love can be still, and be love, still.

Author's Bio

Saul Hillel Benjamin is late to fatherhood, earlier to poetry; earlier still to public service. Five years in the upper reaches of the first Clinton Administration; seven years in conflict resolution and school innovation work in Lebanon and Bosnia and Morocco. Fourteen years leading multicultural and "Great Books" interdisciplinary programs for high schools and universities in the USA and Morocco. Published in *The American Scholar, The Yale Review, BBC-Three, The Christian Science Monitor, Dissent, The American Oxonian, The Poetry Society of Great Britain*, FM 107 Winnipeg, *The 2019 San Diego Poetry Anthology*, and chosen by a U.S. Poet Laureate and a UK Poet Laureate for the *2016 and 2017 Vice Chancellors International Poetry Anthologies*.

Coming Home with Cancer

by

Cameron Morse

for my father, who taught me the love of reading

Table of Contents

Acknowledgments

I am grateful to my wife, Lili, and my son, Theodore. Our adventures together are the inspiration for these poems. I thank my parents for taking me with them to China and China for doing the rest. Many of these poems are familiar to my workshop at Inklings' Books and Coffee Shoppe: Eve Brackenbury, Ariel Diaz, Maija Rhee Devine, K.L. Frank, and Jemshed Khan. I am also grateful to the Creative Writing Program at the University of Missouri—Kansas City and the editors in whose magazines the following poems first appeared (some in earlier forms):

Algebra of Owls: "Requiem for Heavenly Mountain Road," "Looking at My Parents."
The Cresset: "On 'Saint Frances Adoring a Crucifix' by Guido Reni."
Communion Arts Journal: "Anticonvulsant."
Dappled Things: "Comfort Items," "The Cave."
I-70 Review: "Honeymoon in Lijiang."
The Indianapolis Review: "Haiku Sequence on Dexamethasone,"
        "Description of a Typical Day for My Continuing Disability
        Report."
Luna Luna: "Shaving My Head."
New Letters: "The Fitting," "The Phlebotomist," "After the Seizure."
New Madrid: a Journal of Contemporary Literature: "Voices."
Route 7 Review: "GBM SURVIVORS TO THIVERS!"
Sweet Tree Review: "The Color of China."
Visitant: "Poe Poem."
Visions International: "The Names of Paint."

Requiem for Heavenly Mountain Road

*We can so easily find that we are trapped, as in a dream
and die there, without ever waking up.*
        —Rainer Maria Rilke

In a factory park on the outskirts of Yantai,
I would walk around talking to God—*Father who art
in heaven*—and you,
my earthly father, I walked along Heavenly Mountain Road
with you, talking to the charcoal sky.

While you texted one of six women, I spoke to the windbreaks,
the dark winter tide. Like Rilke,
I feared I wasn't really living. On the night
of my first seizure, I knew I had to die to bring you back
to my bedside.

But Dad, I weary of waiting.
If you aren't coming, I will take your place at the kitchen counter.
I will pick paper jackets off the cloves of garlic, slice onion
and scoop seeds out of spaghetti squash. I will feed your family
in your stead. I will feed your godforsaken children.

After the Seizure

When I could still dribble, my left hand flapped to the stop sign and back.
It steadied the basketball over my forehead.
On Dexamethasone, I could still type

with both hands. In this way
I spent the last summer of my life shooting baskets in the driveway
and typing dark, ecstatic lines.

Afterwards, my right hand learned to cover the full court
of the keyboard while its teammate dangled
like a jacket. Shortening muscles

drew my left arm into my chest. My physical therapist laid me out
and taught me stretches, the tenderness
with which I would have to bring my left hand back to its senses.

Autumn Thoughts

These lovely seasons and fragrant years falling
lonely away—we share such emptiness here.
      —Po Chü-i

Without him in the house he half owns, we share in
our father's emptiness, a vacancy
through which other men pass, tightening screws,
changing lightbulbs, talking politics.

Spider webs drag over bare arms the lineaments
of the invisible man who lives with us.
They frame his absence in the orchard
where crab apple trees raise amputated limbs,

the bitten leaves of our lives a memorandum
to emptiness. A polka dotted woodpecker
bangs its head, drumming like a downspout
in the rain, knuckles rapping on the front door,

abandoned adult children eyeing the stranger
on tippy toe through the peephole. Every day,
the mailwoman slaps shut the mailbox lid.
More letters come for him—the gone man,

his dead parents and married daughter—
than for those of us who are left with autumn
thoughts, picking a barefoot path through
the driveway's minefield of broken acorns.

The Fitting

On my first visit to the Department
of Radiology, my therapist slips

a sheet of plastic into her stainless
steel basin. I close my eyes

while she drapes its wet
weave over my face, the limp

latticework adhering
to cheekbone. I lie upon her table

like a corpse getting dressed
in a funeral parlor.

She smooths out the wrinkles
in my skin. Her cool fingers trace

the contours of my eyelids, molding
a face out of warm water.

All right, all finished, she says,
peeling off the hardened semblance

of myself, a cerecloth full of breathing holes,
porous membrane still dripping.

Later, the mask bolts my head to the cot.
It clutches my skull.

Her machine arm swivels loud, invisible
beams into my brain.

Honeymoon in Lijiang

I remember the glitter of the killing
stone, the scales silver

and swimming bladder pink,
beached in wet crags,

what kept the carp afloat
floating. We fought,

slept, and made love in the shadow
of Jade Snow Dragon Mountain.

Somewhere among the pines
in a ravine called Aroma

of Horse Droppings,
we ran across a man whose job

it was to confiscate
cigarette lighters. No fires

allowed among the inflammatory cones.
He left with our names.

He left us aflame, to stay late
watching hawks bank

above the terracotta rooftops
of Old Town, to lay down

in a bed of pine needles
and discover each other's handles.

We fought, slept, and made love
so close to heaven

we could hear the clouds whisper
incantations over the ground.

Looking at My Parents

*Those who do not see the flower are no different from barbarians, and
those who do not imagine the moon are akin to beasts.*
—Bashō

When I look at my father, I see a flower,
I see a barbarian who lived in Guam
and ate McDonald's for 90 days to file
for divorce. When I look at my father,
I see a flower wearing a straw hat, short
shorts and long socks, t-shirt tucked,
stretched over his paunch, I see a bottle
of wine with a hamburger for breakfast
before going back to bed. I see red
meat and liver-spotted hands.

When I look at my mother, I see the moon,
I see a beast who watches *Call the Midwife*
in her nightgown, indulging herself
and 16-year-old son with a weight problem
to Custard's after a day in the office
listening to sex addicts and divorcées
before getting served on September 11th
by what she thought had been a rooter with a bid.
When I look at my mother, I see the moon,
haggard and luminous.

Shaving My Head

I rake the ridges
of my skull.

Sickles rasp
across my scalp,

carving corridors
through a snowscape

of shaving cream.
When my radiologist

says the Beam
could turn my hair

a different color,
I don't ask which

or even if it will
grow back

in patches like a dog
with mange.

Dad's hair darkened
into his thirties,

Holy Ghosting
with age.

I'd take firetruck
red or go

platinum blond,
if it would mean a few

more months,
or one good poem.

GBM SURVIVORS TO THIRVERS!

She says her husband doesn't make it to the bathroom.
She says her husband stares at himself
in the bathroom mirror at midnight. When he comes back,
he just stands there looking down at the indentation
his body made beside her.

Does this mean the tumor's grown, she asks,
or is it because of the weaning, the gradual reduction
of anti-inflammatories? Out the bay window,
snow is falling. Around the kitchen table,
people chatter about substituting cranberries

for marshmallows in the baked yams, the benefits maple
syrup over brown sugar, and what about fresh green beans
instead of canned? Recipes for stuffed mushrooms,
blending batter for pumpkin pancakes. I sink
into my captain's chair, cradling coffee in both hands.

Outside the snow shifts like static, the signal interrupted.
People chatter about substituting the chain links
for new pickets. Setting the posts in cement.
Getting started Wednesday. Renting the augur, breaking out
the reciprocating saw. People chatter. Snow unloads

more snow out the bay window, more and more
snow out of the sky's dark wardrobe.

The Cave

Vampire you call me, leaving for work,
me at home on SSI, unemployed.

Vampire for shutting the door to my study,
for lowering the blinds, for sucking,

sucking you dry: my cook,
my bank. My wife you're right.

I'm not the man you married anymore:
that man with the black scab

flaking like snow above his incised
right hemisphere, stretchmarks on his legs

like smudges of purple lipstick, neck
beard grown grizzly and temple shagged

around the bald crown of his head
does not remind me of myself.

But it is me—quarantined to the basement,
on the chemo couch drained, watching

daytime TV—Jerry Springer my only light source.
Other than you, of course. You hold me

upright so that I can see the screen,
you help me up the steps, baby steps,

into your icicled birdbath, your sky
full of falling leaves.

The Color of China

The grass is blue about the river
that runs around my teacup,
but so are the pagodas, footbridges,
the fishermen and their sampans.

The warped willows flourish their vines
like freshly dipped quills, dripping blue
with ink of the decal, a vortex
wrapped around the world, a whirlpool

of porcelain, like a doll's head
sawn off at the hairline, a coffee-stained
basin of bone. Believe me,
I would tell you if the grass in Beijing

were blue, but its roadside shag is
as white as the slender hand of the mistress
courtesan. Dump truck dust powders
every blade, and smog absconds

with the sun on so many winter days,
I drown my sorrows like her sot
husband, returning
from his revels to find himself alone.

Poe Poem

Because of the mask that molded to my face
during the fitting, hardening as the warm water dried,
the mask that fastened my head to the cot,
and because of the cot that carried me into the machine,
the BEAM that unloaded a single dose
of radiation every morning, Monday through Friday,
and because the techs left me alone in there
to take my dose, closing the steel door behind them,
while the robot arm rotated
around my head, firing invisible shots of radiation,
I wrote no poems. I had no thoughts.
The radiologist said I would be dead within two years.
Ravens decorated the ceiling panels. I read
"The Masque of the Red Death" on rides to the Department
of Radiology, pulling down my stocking cap
over my ears. I shaved my head,
grew out my beard. For the first time in my life,
I insisted on carving jack-o'-lanterns,
clawing out the cold slime of their brains
with my fingernails.

Father Christmas

for Ariel Diaz

Snow fleshes out the ribcages
of unraked oak leaves, wood pile

whitening like the dog's winter coat.
Makes me wonder if it's snowing in Yantai,

snowing over the Bohai Sea, where you live
with your new family called Forget, called Spirits,

called Loneliness. I remember your shaking
hands that last Christmas I visited.

Shaking with anger or Parkinson's, you thought
only of Parkinson's, women,

a shot of heroin to use in case of another
heart attack. That last walk

we took along the frozen coast, you were zipped
like a lumberjack in coveralls

and earmuffs. Looking back, I know
my tumor nestled even then

inside me, glial white in gray
matter, while our heartfelt debates about God

and the family garbage gave way
to the tick of snowflakes.

The Names of Paint

How about Summer's End, for the summer in which we met,
the summer that has lasted ten years now?
Or a gallon of Steelyard Common

after the construction site that dusted the ashes and locusts
at Beijing New Talent? Cricket,
for early autumn walks around the dormitories,

glowing like shuttlecraft in the hedgerow silence
of dead cicadas? Tea Leaves for the glass thermoses
refilled between classes at scalding

silver faucets, Cliveden Gray Morning
for the thickening smog, smother of ectoplasm,
for particulate matter infiltrating the bloodstream.

Not Belle Groove Fog, but Mucous Green, for phlegm
hawked upon the train station platform, Floral White for the gauze
mask pinched to your nose bridge, steaming my glasses.

Comfort Items

This morning's lawn is cluttered
with fallen branches, the clumps of new
maple and oak leaves like hair
dropped during chemo. Mom—staying

home from church to come down
after a week of counseling hoarders,
control freaks, meth heads and their legal
guardians—heads out into the dark rain.

Hearing the lid bang open the COUNTY DISPOSAL can,
I drop the poem I'm working on, take up
the nearest stocking cap and rain
jacket, and join her in the boneyard of wet

moss-eaten branches, the pink skullcap
on my head, like the green and yellow afghan,
one of the comfort items from *Cancer Action*
that she collected on my behalf.

Resection Cavity

On Mom's birthday,
the day she completes her second lap,
surpassing my years times two,
another mother's son has his tumor
removed. Afterwards, he won't
remember her name. His resection
cavity will be cavernous, the mouth
of the cave agape. Imagined
as an inkblot, it retains the substance
of ink. As a blackbird, feathers,
talons and perhaps a beak, but
as a cavity the white enamel of him
cradles emptiness, the dark
hollow of a tree, the way she cradled
him night long after her husband
rolled over like a stone
and fell back asleep. Cradled him
until his hysteria subsided,
and lowered the warm bundle
over the crib rail, the hollow
within her slowly closing.

The Phlebotomist

Don't look, she says,
as the butterfly needle slips

into the crook of my arm,
but I can't help watching

her silver proboscis
pierce the bruise

of weekly blood draws,
the blue blossom

of scar tissue, or how she
hovers above me

like a seamstress searching
for a seam, threading

herself into my bloodstream.
Don't look, she says.

What she means is, if you flinch,
I might miss. I might slip.

I might kiss you, by accident.

Description of a Typical Day for My Continuing Disability Report

On a typical day, I wake up with cancer,
spoon coconut oil onto polymer.
My iceberg of healthy natural fat pirouettes
above a spreading puddle.

If my cancer cells require glucose, I give them
ketones. I beat ketones into my eggs.
On a typical day I drink six cups of coffee,
pouring them out of my thermos, little
by little, into stoneware. I reserve
the morning of a typical day for psalms

of blastoma, the songs of my cells, an uncontrollable
division of angels on the head of a pin, the tip
of a needle. I fill Moleskine after Moleskine
with the concrete details of a typical day,
its dishes hot out of the washing machine,
the smell of laundry in the nostril
of the exhaust fan, a rusty spade left out in the rain.

After Bashō

How odd that what started as an amusement
can turn into a lifelong business.

Now that I am not expected to live long,
I patrol the side yard, attuned to the trill of early autumn.

What pursuit is this that leads me daily
outside myself? As if I could stand in the stream,

untouched by traffic because a stereotactic needle
kissed my forehead.

In this mortal frame of mind, you said,
there's something windswept.

So be it. Let neither hope nor despair
deprive us of today's bedraggled phloxes,

the black eyeballs of those who have dropped the pursuit.
Let's forget ourselves completely

in lieu of acorns, their burst integuments
streaking in the driveway like the tails of comets.

Haiku Sequence on Dexamethasone

Wake up, 3 o'clock dark
kneecaps coruscating.

Stagger from chair back
to countertop.

At Walmart, ask
for a bottle of Jim Beam.

Night crew sliding
boxcutters through packing tape,
glass cabinet locked.

*

Weep in bathroom stall
of Blue Springs 8
Theatre

after watching *The Giver.*

*

Plant ornamental pear.

Guideposts hammered
into the earth, nails
in a coffin.

Falling down, they cross
each other like fingers.

*

Limp home along Golfview
Road with bag of Chex
Mix, wrapped

in constellations of pain, barbed
wire of starlight.

On "Saint Francis Adoring a Crucifix" by Guido Reni

Last night, at Inklings'
Books and Coffee Shoppe,

when you asked if I am ever going
to stop writing cancer poems

and pursue other subjects, I thought
of Saint Francis tonsured

at the Nelson-Atkins,
his cadaverous hands folded

over his breast like wings, how the right
hand rests upon the left, as if

to perform CPR on his own stopped
heart, the breath sucked out

of his lungs, his eyes flung open
at the moment of arrest, the moment

arrested, and may you never know
what it's like to be transfixed,

to don a stitched cassock and waft
like a dove in the updraft, caught up

in the representation of a death
which is also your own.

Anticonvulsant

Little tablet,
sky-blue

sacrament, paint
chip off the ceiling

of a cathedral,
I call you Keppra,

my Protector:
Levetiracetam.

Twice daily
your splinter

of stained glass
passes through the palm

of my hand.
Twice daily I accept

your gospel of 250 ml.
Transubstantiate

your body into my
blood, your word

into my flesh.
I accept

your side effects:
somnolence,

decreased energy,
suicide, salvation.

Voices

"Not that you could endure God's voice—far from it. But listen to the voice of the wind / And the ceaseless message that forms itself out of silence."
—Rainer Maria Rilke

When I listen to the voice of the wind instead of God's
what I hear is a hiss in the oak leaves like rice
pouring into an empty pot. It makes sense

that I would be alone during the seizure
in which I swallow my tongue, alone and unable
to call anyone to roll over my body.

It makes sense that I'd be alone during the eclipse
and voiceless in the silence of swallows flown
home from the soybean fields. Nightfall came early for me,

too. I knew it was night when my shadow crawled
back into my body and a chill slipped
like black lace into the wind.

Author's Bio

Cameron Morse lives with his wife Lili and son Theodore in Blue Springs, Missouri. He was diagnosed with a glioblastoma in 2014. With a 14.6 month life expectancy, he entered the Creative Writing program at the University of Missouri–Kansas City and, in 2018, graduated with an M.F.A. His poems have been published in numerous magazines, including *New Letters, Bridge Eight,* and *South Dakota Review.* His first collection, *Fall Risk,* won Glass Lyre Press's 2018 Best Book Award. His second, *Father Me Again,* is available from Spartan Press.

Critical Praise

Blevins's poems shepherd us through her speakers' innermost territories—their hillsides and ravines. We experience lust's undeniable electricity, the anguish of the abandoned, motherhood's trials. In *Susurration,* complex moments spread over the pages like wounds, as with this painful challenge: "Memorize the sound of laughter / exploding from the mouth /of a lover at great distance: a clasp's / hook letting go of its eye." We understand that many lines in these poems are not mere pleas or lamentations, but works of magic and healing.—Elijah Burrell, author of *Troubler* and *The Skin of the River*

With equal parts tenderness and fierceness, Blevins shares startlingly original and courageous poetry that simmers and shimmers with susurration: a word that truly sounds like the whispering, rustling, and murmuring it is. "A mother was a child once without love. She calls the earth a person. / In the beginning, no one needed to be told how to become a person," Blevins writes in this remarkable collection of embodied poems, each one a shining and searing exploration of how to love, live, and be a woman and mother. What we as readers hear and see here are deep forays into love and loss, grief and gratitude, motherhood and loverhood, all kindled by the fire of women loving women. Altogether, these poems speak to the pain, pleasure, and possibilities of such love and with the embodied wisdom of living that love. —Caryn Mirriam-Goldberg, author of *Miriam's Well*

"To keep loving where wonderfully/we once ached in love is not easy" begins "The Anniversary of Everyday" by Benjamin, a poet who is as talented as he is needed. In these sincere yet unsentimental poems, readers are gifted with something rare to find: admissions of sadness, celebration, and the uneasy twine that bridges the two. With carefully crafted allusions, rhythms, and figurative language, these poems are works of a true artist. "December Weather", for example, is as good a poem as any contemporary poet would hope to ever write. To declare the potential of living "with the loyalty of our including hearts" may well be a commentary on our world's present shortcomings as it is a testament of wounded but insightful private love".—Charlotte Pence, author of *Many Small Fires*

"A true poet must have the ability, to borrow a phrase from Dryden, "to charm the ear." Benjamin has this talent in abundance. His deeply felt poems celebrating fatherhood, friendship and nature strike a perfect balance of sentiment and irony. Like the famous violins that inspire his "Stradivari" suite, Benjamin's poems keep the secrets of their magic while weaving their spell on us. There is such wonderful music in these poems. And the title poem "Laud", a new kind of sonnet with subtle skill, is so good that I can hear the praise of The Nine Ladies for its power and grace".—Daniel Mark Epstein, author of *Dawn to Twilight: Selected Poems.*

Morse confronts hard truths and transforms them. These poems offer readers faith in life and in art—a medical diagnosis and the clinical procedures that it involves can be shoved aside. We have here a poet whose craft and strength of will proceed toward beauty, family, and birth. These poems grow in stature and distinction by elevating seemingly mundane details of life. Instead of listening only, and merely, to God's voice in the wind, Morse says, "I hear / a hiss in the oak leaves / like rice pouring into an empty pot." Such stunning imagery allows us readers to live more intensely. Morse is a gifted poet, whose poems are a gift to the rest of us. —Robert Stewart, author of *Working Class.*

More from BLP

Delphi Series Vol. **1**

Anna Leahy
Karen L. George
Robert Perry Ivey

Delphi Series Vol. **2**

Joy Ladin
Jennifer Litt
Tasha Cotter

Delphi Series Vol. **3**

Aaron Bauer
Francine Rubin
Meghan Sterling

Delphi Series Vol. **4**

Ting Gou
Claire Zoghb
Erin Redfern

Delphi Series Vol. **5** (fiction)

Diane Payne
Lana Spendl
Chella Courington

Delphi Series Vol. **6**

Allison Blevins
Saul Hillel Benjamin
Cameron Morse

Delphi Series Vol. **7** (forthcoming)

Marjorie Power
Sally Zakariya
Martha McCollough

Delphi Series Vol. **8** (forthcoming)

Charlette Mandel
Carly Sachs
Lois Marie Harrod

www.ingramcontent.com/pod-product-compliance
Lightning Source LLC
Chambersburg PA
CBHW051816040426
42446CB00007B/692